Strengthening Your
Faith

Other Women of Faith Bible Studies

WOMEN OF FAITH℠
BIBLE STUDY SERIES

Strengthening Your
Faith

Written by
BEVERLY WILSON

General Editor
TRACI MULLINS

ZondervanPublishingHouse
Grand Rapids, Michigan

A Division of HarperCollins*Publishers*

Strengthening Your Faith
Copyright © 1998 by Women of Faith, Inc.

Requests for information should be addressed to:

ZondervanPublishingHouse
Grand Rapids, Michigan 49530

ISBN: 0-310-21337-1

General Editor, Traci Mullins
Cover and interior illustration by Jim Dryden
Interior design by Sue Vandenberg Koppenol

Printed in the United States of America

98 99 00 01 02 03 04 /❖ EP/ 10 9 8 7 6 5 4 3 2 1

Thanks . . .
There is, most of all, my Lord,
there is my priceless family,
there are my treasured friends;
but this thanks is for my son, Brent.
How blessed am I
that God chose me to be your mom
and you to be my son.
I love you most!

CONTENTS

FOREWORD

The best advice I ever received was in 1955. I was twenty-three. Somebody had the good sense to say to me, "Luci, if you want to give yourself a gift, learn all you can about the Bible. Start going to a Bible class and don't stop until you have some knowledge under your belt. You won't be sorry." Having just graduated from college, I was living with my parents, and together we drove more than twenty miles to attend that class. We went four nights a week for two years. I've *never* been sorry.

Nothing I've ever done or learned has meant more to me than those classes. Unless I was on my deathbed, I didn't miss. I went faithfully, took notes, absorbed everything like a sponge, asked questions relentlessly, and loved *every* minute! (I probably drove the teacher crazy.)

Today, more than forty years later, this wonderful storehouse of truth is my standard for living, giving, loving, and learning. It is my Rock and Fortress, the pattern for enjoying abundant life on earth, and for all eternity. I know what I believe, and why. I'm open to change on my tastes, personal opinions, even some of my choices. But change my biblical convictions? No way! They're solid and secure, based on God's inerrant, enduring, and unchanging Word. There's nothing like learning God's truth. As he says, it sets you free.

Women of Faith Bible studies are designed to help you deal with everyday problems and issues concerning you. Experienced and wise women who, like the rest of us, want to know God intimately, have written these lessons. They encourage us to dig into the Scriptures, read them carefully, and respond to thought-provoking questions. We're invited to memorize certain verses as sources of support and guidance, to hide his Word in our heads and hearts.

The clever ideas in these studies make me smile. The stories move my spirit. There are valuable suggestions in dealing with others, quotations that cause me to stop and think. The purpose of every activity is to put "some knowledge under your belt" about the Bible and its relevance for life *this very day.*

Give yourself a gift. Grab your Bible, a pencil, notepad, cup of coffee . . . maybe even a friend . . . and get started. I assure you—you'll *never* be sorry.

LUCI SWINDOLL

HOW TO USE THIS GUIDE

Women of Faith Bible studies are designed to take you on a journey toward a more intimate relationship with Christ by bringing you together with your sisters in the faith. We all want to continue to grow in our Christian lives, to please God, to be a vital part of our families, churches, and communities. But too many of us have tried to grow alone. We haven't found enough places where we feel safe to share our heartaches and joys and hopes. We haven't known how to support and be supported by other women in ways that really make a difference. Perhaps we haven't had the tools.

The guide you are about to use will give you the tools you need to explore a fundamental aspect of your walk with God *with* other women who want to grow, too. You'll not only delve into Scripture and consider its relevance to your everyday life, but you'll also get to know other women's questions, struggles, and victories—many similar, some quite different from your own. This guide will give you permission to be yourself, to share honestly, to care for one another's wounds, and laugh together when you take yourselves too seriously.

Each of the six lessons in this guide is divided into six sections. Most you'll discuss as a group; others you'll cover on your own during the week between meetings.

A Moment for Quiet Reflection. The questions in this section are meant to be answered in a few minutes of privacy sometime before you join your group each week. You may already carve out a regular time of personal reflection in your days, so you've experienced the refreshment and insight these times bring to your soul. However, if words like "quiet," "reflection," and "refreshment" have become unfamiliar to you, let this guide get you started with the invaluable practice of setting aside personal time to think, to rest, to pray. Sometimes the answers you write down to the questions in this section will be discussed as a group when you come together; other times they'll just give you something to ponder deep within. Don't neglect this important reflection time each week, and include enough time to read the introduction to the lesson so you'll be familiar with its focus.

Knowing God's Heart. The questions in this section will take you into the Bible, where you and the women in your group can discover God's heart and mind on the subject at hand. You'll do the Bible study together, reading the Scriptures aloud and sharing your understanding of the passage so all of you can learn together what God has to say about your own heart and life, right now. While you don't need to complete the study questions prior to each group session, it will be helpful for you to read through this part of the lesson beforehand so you can begin thinking about your answers. There is a lot to cover in each lesson, so being somewhat familiar with the content before your meetings will save your group time when you actually do your study together.

Friendship Boosters. A big part of why you've come together is to deepen your friendships with other women and to support each other in meaningful ways. The questions and activities in this section are designed to link you together in bonds of friendship, faith, and joy. Whether you are meeting the other women in your group for the first time or are old friends, this section will boost the quality and pleasure in your relationships as well as give you opportunities to support each other in practical ways.

Just for Fun. God's plan for our lives certainly isn't all work and no play! Central to being a woman of faith is cultivating a joyful spirit, a balanced perspective, and an ability to enjoy life because of God's faithfulness and sovereignty. Every week you'll be given an idea or activity that will encourage you to enjoy your journey, laugh, and lighten your load as you travel the path toward wholehearted devotion together.

Praying Together. Nothing is more important than asking God to help you and your friends as you learn how to live out his truths in your lives. Each time you get together you'll want to spend some time talking to him about your individual and mutual concerns.

Making It Real in Your Own Life. You'll respond to these questions or activities on your own after group meetings, but don't consider them just an afterthought. This section is critical because it will help you discover more ways to apply what you've learned and discussed to your own life in the days and weeks ahead. This section will be a key to making God's liberating truths more real to you personally.

In each section, space is provided after each question for you to record your answers, as well as thoughts stimulated by others' answers during group discussion. While you can gain wisdom from completing parts of this guide on your own, you'll miss out on a lot of the power—and the fun!—of making it a group experience.

One woman should be designated as the group facilitator, but she needn't have any training in leading a Bible study or discussion group. The facilitator will just make sure the discussion stays on track, and there are specific notes to help her in the "Leader's Guide" section at the back of this book. Keeping your group size to between four and eight participants is ideal because then it will be possible for everyone to share each week. The length of time you'll need to complete the lessons together will depend largely on how much the participants talk, so the group facilitator will need to monitor the time to keep it under ninety minutes. The facilitator can also speed up or slow down the group time by choosing to skip some discussion questions or concentrate longer on others. If you decide to do this study in a larger group or Sunday school class, split up into smaller groups for discussion. Especially make sure no one gets left out of the process of building friendships and having fun!

Now that you've studied the map, your journey should go smoothly. Celebrate being women of faith as you travel together. *Enjoy!*

INTRODUCTION
Simple Faith

Faith. That intangible, indescribable, indispensable ingredient without which we can't know Jesus or please God. Just what is faith anyway? "It's simple," explained my eleven-year-old son, Brent. "It's what you believe even though you can't see it." Well, it does say something like that in the Bible . . . but simple?

If faith is supposed to be simple—or childlike, as the Bible implies in Matthew 18:3—why do we struggle so to have it? We fight to identify faith and then to get it and then to hold on to it. Is it really even available? Where do we sign up for it? Maybe it's on back order and we need a rain check!

It was Jesus himself who said we just needed to have faith the size of a mustard seed—one of the smallest seeds there is—and then we could watch its incredible progress as it grows into one of the biggest trees around. If such a small amount is really all that's required, it seems like we should be able to scrape that together, doesn't it?

Does the size of your own faith make that mustard seed look like the moon: too big for personal use and too far away to reach by the conventional means available to you? And do these people in the Bible really know anything about faith that can help you today? I mean, after all, God included them in his Book, so they must be stellar examples—which puts them right up there with that unattainable moon-sized faith.

If these questions ring a bell for you, don't file that rain check away in the back of a drawer just yet! This study will help you see that faith is a process as much as it is a product, the journey as well as the destination.

We will be looking at six different women of the Bible and the type of faith each one exhibited. Although they were all women of God, they were also very human. They laughed and cried, they waited on God, and they impatiently "helped" him along. They were an example to those around them and are an encouragement to us.

As you get to know these women whom God included in the Bible to teach and inspire us, and as you get to know the women he chose to be in this study group for you to grow with and pray for, you will find that faith, "being sure of what we hope for and certain of what we do not see" (Heb. 11:1), is a shield (Eph. 6:16) that you too can sport victoriously!

The Woman of Ill Repute: Extravagant Faith

Have you ever noticed that a wrapped bandage or medication sample often carries the warning, "Guaranteed sterile until opened"? I always wonder if the manufacturer is trying to insinuate that it is better not to open the package at all! But an unopened bandage is unable to do what it was designed to do; it is of no use to anyone.

It is like that with faith. If you keep it packaged up and so private that no one else knows about it, it is sterile and useless. But if you are willing to unwrap your faith you will fill the air with its sweet perfume and it will be a blessing to you, to those around you, and to the Lord Jesus himself.

In Luke 7:36–50 we see a beautiful picture of faith released, and the release it in turn brings. The scene is a dinner at the home of a Pharisee, one of those holier-than-thou sharks with whom Jesus had little patience. In comes a woman who had been a prostitute. Now Pharisees and prostitutes mix like the proverbial oil and water, but she came because she had heard Jesus was there, and nothing would keep her away from him, in whom was forgiveness and peace. She braved the scorn of the Pharisee and his other guests because she possessed an extravagant faith in Jesus that she was compelled to express. She held nothing back from him and, as she poured out her most costly material possession at Jesus' feet, she filled the room with the aroma of her praise.

As you read the story let it inspire you to set the fragrance of your faith free, and then encourage the others in your group to do the same.

> *Faith is response to*
> *Love's dear call,*
> *Of Love's dear face the sight;*
> *To do Love's bidding*
> *now is all*
> *That gives the heart delight.*
> *To love Thy voice*
> *and to reply,*
> *"Lord, here am I."*
>
> HANNAH HURNARD

A Moment
for Quiet Reflection

1. Think about your most precious possession. How would your being willing to give it up for Jesus reflect an extravagant faith?

2. Read Matthew 6:19–21. What kind of treasure are you storing up for yourself? What are some ways you could "give" your treasure on earth to Jesus?

Knowing God's Heart

1. Read Luke 7:36–50 together. As Jesus is dining at the home of Simon the Pharisee, a most startling incident occurs. Even had she been invited, which she decidedly was not, an ex-prostitute coming into the Pharisee's home and anointing Jesus in such a way was startling in itself. The reaction of Jesus, however, was even more surprising. Why? What impact did it have—not only on the woman that day, but on all women, including you?

2. The Pharisees prided themselves on being righteous and keeping the law of Moses. They were considered the spiritual leaders of their day. Yet in this scene, the sinful woman exhibits the greatest faith in and devotion to Jesus. What are the key differences between the woman and the Pharisee?

3. Take a look at the different characters in this narrative: Simon the Pharisee, the sinful woman anointing Jesus' feet with her tears and perfume, the two men who owed money in Jesus' story, and Simon's other guests. With whom do you most identify and why?

4. Why do you think the woman went to Jesus?

5. What would you have to overcome to approach Jesus with such abandon?

6. How do you suppose Jesus' gracious response to the sinful woman affected her?

7. Think of a time which, as you look back on it, called for a display of extravagant faith. Share with the group whether you expressed that kind of faith or if your faith looked more like that of Simon and his friends. What were the results of your response?

8. Would you do anything differently if a similar situation came up in the future? If so, what?

9. Consider a situation in your life today that calls for greater faith on your part. What would you want Jesus to say to you today that would encourage you in an extravagant faith in him?

> *The greatest joy is not in receiving, but in giving from our one-of-a-kind hearts. When we get outside ourselves enough to let God's life flow through us, the sweet fruit of his Spirit will grow and nourish everyone around us.*
>
> BARBARA JOHNSON

Friendship Boosters

1. Your group leader will hand out name tags. On the back is her name and number. As she hands you your name tag, introduce yourself and share your phone number with the group. As the other women introduce themselves, write down their names and numbers on the back of your name tag.

2. Discuss what holds you back from an extravagant faith, those things you are keeping to yourself. Write down one of those to "pour out" at Jesus' feet and pass the paper to the woman on your left. During the week, pray for and call the woman whose paper you received and encourage her in her lavish faith.

Just for Fun

1. What is your favorite fragrance? Fresh pine? Chanel No. 5? Laundry dried in the sun and wind? Chocolate chip cookies? Talk about why an extravagant faith would smell like your favorite scent.

2. Write out your favorite verse about "faith." Attach it to a small, fragrant gift (for instance, a scented votive candle, a perfume sample, a flower, a fresh cookie or muffin) and bring it to the group next week.

Praying Together

Join in a "round-robin" prayer. Beginning with your group leader, go around the circle and offer a one-sentence prayer of praise to the Lord. The second time around, pray a sentence about what you are hoping for in this group over the next several weeks. The third time around, pray that the woman whose paper you received would be able to "pour out" at Jesus' feet that which holds her back from living out an extravagant faith. Your leader will start each new round and will close your prayer time with a final sentence of blessing.

> *Common sense is not faith, and faith is not common sense; they stand in the relation of the natural and the spiritual; of impulse and inspiration.*
>
> OSWALD CHAMBERS

Making It Real
in Your Own Life

1. Consider one specific way in which you can express an extravagant faith in Jesus in the week ahead. Write down what comes to mind, and make a plan to follow through.

2. Pray a short prayer for extravagant faith each day this week. Try praying within "sniffing distance" of the scent you used to describe your faith in "Friendship Boosters." (You might have to get creative if your favorite scent isn't readily available!) Whenever you smell that fragrance in your daily life, pray and ask God how he wants you to live out an extravagant faith.

The highest response to anyone who lavishes redemptive, unconditional love on us is to return that love and please the person in every way possible.
CYNTHIA HEALD

LESSON TWO

Elizabeth: Intimate Faith

I love T-shirts with clever sayings. Not to wear, mind you, just to admire! One of my favorites is a shirt that states in tiny letters over the left pocket, "INTROVERT." Would an introvert feel that even this small declaration attracted too much attention to herself? Perhaps an extrovert would wear it just for the laugh and the attention! How about you: do you consider yourself to be an introvert or an extrovert?

It is common to think of an introvert as a shy person and an extrovert as an outgoing person. While these traits may indeed be characteristic of these personality types, a truer determining factor is a person's answer to the question "How are you revitalized: by being alone or by being with other people?" Introverts may or may not be shy, quiet, wallflower types, but when their batteries want recharging they need to be by themselves. Likewise, extroverts may or may not be gregarious, outgoing, exuberant folks, but when they want to be reenergized they need to be with people.

Regardless of whether believers are introverts or extroverts by nature, they need to spend time alone with God to grow and be renewed in their relationship with him. Consider the closest relationships in your life; they are undoubtedly with people with whom you are able to spend time

26

alone, one-to-one, whether in person or via the phone or the mail, to really get to know each other. It's the same with God. If you know him only in the context of the church body or a Bible study group or family prayers at home, then you are missing out on a precious and vital facet of your relationship with him. You can't know him intimately or learn his will and plan for your life unless you spend time with him, just the two of you.

Jesus spent hours and hours alone with his Father, praying and being refreshed and encouraged. And, while he certainly didn't live a life of ease and leisure, he wasn't stressed out and overbooked and frazzled. Rather, he was able to accomplish all that the Father set before him and then declare on the cross, "It is finished."

Elizabeth was the mother of John the Baptist. She and her husband, Zechariah, were well along in years and she was barren when, by a miracle, she became pregnant with John. Let's take a closer look at Elizabeth and try to discover the benefits she reaped from the time she spent alone with the Lord.

> *Perhaps this is the essence of intimacy: not being satisfied or complacent, but always desiring to go deeper into the fullness of God.*
> CYNTHIA HEALD

A Moment
for Quiet Reflection

1. We are so familiar with Psalm 23 as the "funeral psalm."
But now take a few minutes to spend time with the Lord
and reflect on the joyful trust expressed here. Elizabeth
must have known this kind of quiet time with the Lord as
her Shepherd to go through her experience with such
seeming tranquillity. This psalm is a tonic!

2. Write down at least five things our heavenly Shepherd does
for us, according to this psalm. Put these promises in your
own words.

3. What pictures in this psalm particularly spark your desire
to be there with your heavenly Father?

Knowing God's Heart

1. Read Luke 1:5–7 together. What are some things you notice about Elizabeth's faith?

   What kind of woman

2. In Luke 1:11–13 the angel Gabriel visits Zechariah to tell him that his wife will bear a son and they are to name him John. Zechariah has a hard time believing this at first, but Elizabeth does indeed become pregnant. From Luke 1:24–25, what do Elizabeth's words tell us about her beliefs?

   Lord had given her a child reproach.

3. Why do you think she went into seclusion for five months? Keep in mind these were the first five months of her pregnancy, not the last.

4. Do you spend time alone with the Lord? If so, in what specific ways does it affect your faith? (Also consider how your faith is affected if you do not spend time alone with God.)

5. Having children was very important to Israelite women. One reason was that each woman hoped she might be chosen as the mother of the Messiah. From Luke 1:39–45, what do you observe about Elizabeth's response to her young relative, Mary?

6. What do you think this response revealed about Elizabeth's faith?

7. Our faith may or may not stand up to the test when others receive something that we feel should be ours. Briefly tell the group one personal experience you've had along these lines that tested your faith.

8. Read Luke 1:57–63. What does Elizabeth do when her baby is born that, once again, reveals her faith?

Called him John.

9. Think about a time when your faith was questioned or challenged. Were you able to stand firm in your belief? As you tell the group about it, share whether your response was a result of time spent alone with the Lord.

> *God wants you to have a private time with Him,*
> *free from the competition of others. He loves just plain,*
> *simple, exciting you. He wants you all to Himself*
> *to put His loving, divine arms around you.*
> CHARLES STANLEY

Friendship Boosters

1. Break into pairs and give your partner the fragrant gift with verse attached that you brought with you. (Enjoy your gift and meditate on the Scripture in the week ahead.) Then discuss with each other whether or not you enjoy being by yourself and your ideal way of spending time alone. Also discuss how you feel about spending time alone with God. As you come back together as a group, share your partner's response with the other women (it might help to write it down!).

2. Decide when you will spend time alone with the Lord in the week to come, and share with the group what it will take for you to commit to that: the accountability of the group asking you about it next week? Help with your children? Ideas on where and/or how to spend that time? Write down your plan with your name and phone number and pass it to the woman on your left. During the week, pray for the woman whose paper you received and call her to encourage her in her plan.

Just for Fun

Arrange to meet together during the week, ideally in a beautiful place outdoors. Bring your Bibles and read through Psalm 139 together. Then go your separate ways for thirty minutes. While you are by yourself, go through Psalm 139 and meditate on each verse and its implications for your relationship with God today. You might want to write down some thoughts as you savor the quiet and solitude of this brief time. When you all come back together, share your experiences, including how you felt and if having a psalm to think about enriched your time alone with God.

Praying Together

Get back together with your partner and take turns lifting each other up to the Lord. Pray specifically about the plan for time alone with God that your partner outlined for the coming week. Pray that God would remove any obstacles to her plan, and that he would bless her richly in this time.

> *When they saw the courage of Peter and John*
> *and realized that they were unschooled, ordinary men,*
> *they were astonished and they took note that*
> *these men had been with Jesus.*
>
> ACTS 4:13

Making It Real
in Your Own Life

1. Write down your daily "appointment" with God on your calendar this ~~week~~ *month*, even if it's just fifteen or twenty minutes each day. Spend some of the time in prayer and some of it in God's Word, perhaps, for instance, reading a psalm. You might also want to sing a hymn or chorus to him (he's more interested in your heart than the sound of your voice!). You may want to keep some notes about insights that come to you as well as about your experience of being alone with God—everything from quiet alertness to falling asleep! As you do this over time, reread your notes to see how your relationship with God grows in intimacy as you spend time with him and make new discoveries about him.

2. Write out your favorite psalm (to help get you going, check out a few of these: 16, 18, 27, 42, 46, 57, 62, 63, 73, 86, 88, 91, 100, 131, 139, 150), hymn (for instance, "What a Friend We Have in Jesus," "Sweet Hour of Prayer," "I Need Thee Every Hour," "In the Garden," "Rock of Ages"), or chorus (for example, "As the Deer," "Breathe on Me, Breath of God," "As We Seek Your Face," "Seek Ye First"), along with how it encourages you to spend time alone with the Lord.

"Welcome, child," he said.
"Aslan," said Lucy, "you're bigger."
"That is because you are older, little one," answered he.
"Not because you are?"
"I am not. But every year you grow,
you will find me bigger."

C. S. LEWIS

Sarah: Laughing Faith

Does your faith ever inspire you to laugh? Oh, perhaps you have laughed in disbelief at the idea of a heart's desire being fulfilled, but has that laughter become filled with delight as you persisted in faith and watched God make that desire a reality? In between the laughter of doubt and the laughter of faith, how do we continue in faith itself?

Sarah is a picture of this growing faith. Imagine Sarah, or Sarai as she is called when we first meet her. Her name means "princess" and she is the wife of a wealthy man, Abraham. They had a great number of possessions and people when they left Ur and later Haran—both thriving, cultured cities—and they continued to accumulate wealth as they journeyed to Canaan.

Sarai is beautiful as well as wealthy, and here she is, trekking across mideastern deserts because God, whom the people of Ur and Haran neither know nor worship, had called her husband out. Sarai is also barren, but this same God has promised Abram (God changed his name too) that he will make Abram a great nation and that he will have a son. (You can read the wonderful account of this beginning in Genesis 12.) Well, obviously that applies to Sarai as well, and so on they travel, obedient and faithful—for the most part!

But they walk for ten years, and Abram is no more a great nation than he was in Haran, and Sarai is getting older and remains as barren as ever, and maybe they misunderstood God or misinterpreted or did or didn't do something they shouldn't or should have done and . . . oh, the many flaming arrows of the evil one (Eph. 6:16)! We've all felt them, haven't we?

How does Sarah go from laughing skeptically to laughing joyfully? Let's take a closer peek at our princess and our Almighty God, who is faithful despite our faithlessness, and who doesn't give up on us even when we have given up.

> *While I think of God as a pretty efficient guy,*
> *he doesn't always operate in the fast lane. He operates*
> *quite slowly, in fact, when he needs to.*
> MARILYN MEBERG

A Moment
for Quiet Reflection

1. In what situation in your life do you desire or need a laughing, confident faith? Spend a few moments honestly appraising where you are in those circumstances in regard to your faith.

2. Indicate on the spectrum below what your faith looks like in regard to this area. Feel free to add your own words— you know, like "I'm helping God out" (also known as "taking matters into my own hands"), "I'm just hoping for the best" (back of hand dramatically thrown to brow for effect), or "I give up!"

Faith? What faith?   Faith is my middle name!

|——|

3. These days what makes you laugh in doubt? In delight?

Knowing God's Heart

1. Read Genesis 16:1–6 together. After ten years of waiting for God's promise, Sarai resorts to a custom popular in the ancient world: giving her maidservant to her husband in order to have children through her. What evidence, if any, is there that Sarai believed God's earlier promise here?

2. What were the immediate consequences of Sarai's impatience? *Took things into her own hands*

Hagar.   *Gods time or our time*

judgment of Abraham and Sarah

Hard upon Hagar so she fled

3. Discuss at least one way you have taken charge of a situation in which you felt God apparently needed your help, and the outcome when you took control.

4. In Genesis 17:15–17, God changed Sarai's name to Sarah to symbolize that she was called out for his purposes. He also promised Abraham, once again, that he would have a son by Sarah. In Genesis 18:1–15, when three visitors (two angels and evidently the Lord himself) drop in to visit Abraham, Sarah is eavesdropping behind the tent flap when she hears the Lord say that she will have a son by that time next year. How do Abraham and Sarah respond to the reaffirmation of God's earlier promise? Why do you think they responded as they did?

5. Why do you think Sarah was afraid when the Lord asked her husband why she'd laughed?

Laugh - nervous, disbelief

6. Are you ever afraid when God sees your honest position before him, especially when it's full of doubt? Why or why not?

7. Read Genesis 21:1–7. In verses 1 and 2 what three things do we read about the Lord that show he is faithful?

*Visited as he had said
as he had spoken*

8. Abraham and Sarah name their baby boy Isaac because it means "laughter." In verses 6 and 7, how does Sarah sum up what God has done and her feelings about him? (Put her statement of faith in your own words.)

Laugh of Expectation

9. Describe your own faith in a statement or two. What does your definition say about the Lord?

> *He will yet fill your mouth with laughter and*
> *your lips with shouts of joy.*
>
> JOB 8:21

Friendship Boosters

1. If you feel comfortable, briefly share the situation you thought about in your quiet reflection in which you want a laughing, confident faith. If you don't want to share the facts, tell your friends what prevents you from having this kind of faith in these particular circumstances.

2. Talk about what road signs you might see on the next leg of your faith journey if you (a) continue to laugh in disbelief or (b) begin to laugh expectantly now. Sketch one of those road signs on a piece of paper with your name and your situation or the barriers to laughing faith, and pass it to the woman on your right. During the week ahead, pray for the woman whose paper you received, and call her to encourage her. You might even share a laugh of faith!

Just for Fun

1. Using a baby name book (one that includes biblical names and meanings would be great), look up each woman's name and its meaning. Where is God in your name? (For instance, my son's name is Brent Matthew, which means "steep hill" and "gift of God." We have both had to climb a steep hill as I, a single mom, have trained him up. But I know, and I make sure he knows, that he is a gift from the Almighty Lord himself, and that God is right there leading us both up that steep and narrow trail.)

2. Brainstorm ways you can make your name's definition more concrete, or mean something positive if it has a negative connotation. ("Steep hill" isn't exactly encouraging, but it has a connotation of strength; the name itself sounds strong.)

3. Does thinking about your name in a new way help to reframe the situation you discussed with the group? If so, in what way?

[Abraham] a father at 99? Sarah in maternity clothes at 90? They both cackled at the thought. A laugh of ridicule and also of pain. Whatever did [God] want? God wanted faith.... [Abraham] learned to believe when there was no reason left to believe.

PHILIP YANCEY

Praying Together

One at a time, pray for the woman whose road sign you received. Write down the meaning of her name on the road sign. As you pray, ask God to make the meaning of her name, or its positive implication, helpful in her situation (for instance, "Lord, help Brent to grow in strength and endurance as he continues through this school year"). Thank him, also, for one thing that brings you joy or laughter.

Making It Real in Your Own Life

1. Pray for a few minutes, telling God honestly, "I do believe; help me overcome my unbelief!" (Mark 9:24). Decide to take that first small step of faith in having confidence that he will answer your prayer.

2. Begin each day this week by echoing David's prayer, "In the morning, O LORD, you hear my voice; in the morning I lay my requests before you and wait [and laugh!] in expectation" (Ps. 5:3). Present your requests to him and let your "Amen!" ring with expectant laughter as you start the day.

> *Faith, mighty faith, the promise sees*
> *And looks at that alone;*
> *Laughs at impossibilities,*
> *And cries, It shall be done.*
> HANNAH WHITALL SMITH

LESSON FOUR

Ruth: Obedient Faith

When you think of a mother-in-law, you may smile gently and whisper, "Thank you, Lord." This may be a prayer of gratitude for your wonderful mother-in-law . . . or an expression of thankfulness that God has called your mother-in-law to serve in a far-off land . . . or a sigh of relief that you don't have a mother-in-law at all!

In the book of Ruth we meet Ruth's mother-in-law, Naomi. Naomi is an Israelite who, with her husband, Elimelech, and their two sons, Mahlon and Kilion, went from Bethlehem in Judah to live in Moab because of famine. While there, the two sons take Moabite wives, Orpah and Ruth. Although this intermarrying wasn't specifically prohibited, it was not encouraged. (In Deuteronomy 23:3, Moabites were forbidden to enter the assembly of the Lord.)

When the three men subsequently die, the women are left widowed. And when Naomi hears that God has helped his people by providing food for them back home, she decides to return to Bethlehem and urges her daughters-in-law to return to their homes. According to the marriage laws in Israel, the next of kin (usually a brother) was expected to marry the childless widow of his deceased relative. The first child of this new marriage was considered

44

the deceased husband's heir and thus inherited the property and carried on the family name. Naomi points out that she has no other sons, and even if she were to have more sons, the girls would not want to wait until any such males were of marriageable age.

Naomi's daughters-in-law initially protest, but then Orpah's response, although reluctant, is, "Well, if you're sure you'll be all right and don't need me to go with you, well then, I guess I'll head back home. 'Bye, now, take care of yourself, and write when you get settled, okay? Ruth, are you coming? No? Well, have fun and keep in touch!" And we never see or hear of Orpah again.

On the other hand, Ruth's expression of love and devotion to her mother-in-law is an example we still hold up today. While we see a woman of strong character in Naomi, she certainly doesn't appear to be the kind of engaging, fun mother-in-law who might call Ruth and Orpah and say, "Girls! How about we go to the mall and do some shopping and then have a bite of lunch together!" Naomi even calls herself "Marah," meaning *bitterness*. Yet Ruth sees the seed of faith in the true God Almighty rooted within her mother-in-law. Ruth submits her will to God's will in obedience that comes from faith.

Ruth's quiet trust and faith are hallmarks that we see in her obedience throughout the book. We don't see her getting into a tizzy about where to work or how to put food on the table. She follows Naomi's instructions without question. As we study Ruth let's examine our own lives and see how we, too, can live out our faith in active obedience.

> *God has all sorts of unbelievable, wonderful, exciting adventures out there on the horizon of our lives.*
> LUCI SWINDOLL

A Moment
for Quiet Reflection

1. Take a few minutes to read 1 Samuel 15:22, Proverbs 21:3, and Mark 12:28–34. Think honestly about your faith. In what areas is your faith shown through your obedience? In what areas might God want you to grow in faithful obedience to him?

Sam. To oBey better than Sacrifice

2. Write down your favorite verse from above along with a situation in which you want your obedience to reflect your faith. Bring this piece of paper with you to the group meeting this week.

Knowing God's Heart

1. In Ruth 1 we meet Naomi's family, learn of the famine in Judah that drove them to Moab, and see Naomi, Orpah, and Ruth left as widows. We also learn of Naomi's decision to return to Bethlehem when she learns that God has lifted the famine from the land, and we see Orpah's choice to return home as well as Ruth's determination to stay with her mother-in-law. From verses 6–9, what phrases indicate the faith that Ruth recognized in her mother-in-law?

2. Read verses 14–18. What factors do you think influenced Orpah and Ruth's choices?

16

3. As Ruth attempts to express her devotion and determination to stay with Naomi, Orpah is crying and saying goodbye and Naomi is trying to convince Ruth to return to her home. Share with the group a time when you tried—successfully or unsuccessfully—to stand obediently in faith in the face of discouragement.

4. In Ruth 2 we see that Ruth sets out to provide for herself and Naomi, as they have no means of support. The law of Moses allowed for the poor to glean what the harvesters missed from the fields of the landowners. This is where Ruth meets Boaz. In verse 3, Ruth "happens" to end up gleaning in a field belonging to Boaz. Do you think that was a lucky coincidence? Why or why not?

5. Boaz is a man of high standing in the community. We see from his greeting to the harvesters in 2:4 and his words to Ruth in 2:11–12 that he is godly and gracious also. In these verses Boaz uses a beautiful picture of a mother bird gathering her chicks under her wings to describe Ruth's faith in choosing God as her refuge. Share with the group what picture you would like others to see as they observe your faith in the Lord.

6. In Ruth 3 we see Ruth obediently following Naomi's instructions to prepare herself, go down to the threshing floor, and present herself to Boaz. While uncovering his feet may have been simply to cause him to wake in the night, requesting that he spread the corner of his garment over her was most likely intended as a request for marriage (in parts of the Middle East, this custom is still practiced today). Discuss how Ruth's response to Naomi reveals her faith in God.

7. Share with the group an area in your life where your obedience reflects your faith in God. Be as general or specific as you want and as time allows.

8. Boaz assured Ruth that he was flattered by her request and that he would do what he could to honor it. He also explained that while he was a kinsman (with the right to marry his relative's widow and fulfill the law of levirate marriage), there was one that was more closely related who needed to be given first priority in carrying out this obligation. In the morning, he sent Ruth to her mother-in-law with a gift of food. Read 3:16–18. When Ruth returned home and filled her mother-in-law in on the situation, Naomi told her to wait to see how things would turn out. The connotation behind the word "wait" is "sit." Discuss reasons why you think it was or was not difficult for Ruth to sit and rest until the matter was settled.

9. Think of a situation in which you are "waiting on the Lord." What specific things do you learn from Ruth's faith that can help you wait well?

10. In Ruth 4, Boaz took care of the nearer kinsman, who didn't want to jeopardize his own estate by marrying Ruth. Read verse 13, which sums up the Lord's blessing and reward to Ruth because of her obedient faith. Why do you think the birth of Obed was so significant?

11. Read verses 14–22. How did Ruth's marriage and the birth of Obed change Naomi's situation once again and become a source of blessing to her? Why are they important to us today?

12. What are some ways God has blessed your obedience and faith? Discuss how it might impact your family's future.

> *Faith is an action word. Faith is active, not passive.*
> *Faith takes a stand. Faith makes a move. Faith speaks up.*
> *Faith and action are inseparable.*
>
> NEIL ANDERSON

Friendship Boosters

1. If there are "coincidences" happening in your life right now, discuss together how they could be a sign of God's hand in your situation. Sometimes it's easier to see how God is at work when we have others' insight to sharpen our vision.

2. It has been said that faith is a verb. Take out the piece of paper on which you answered the second question in "A Moment for Quiet Reflection." Write down one action that you are going to take in the coming week in obedient response to your faith in God. Make sure your name and phone number are on your paper. Then hand your watch to the leader. (If you're not wearing a watch, then a bracelet, pin, earring, or pen will do.) The leader will put all the items in a basket and walk around the circle, letting each woman draw an item (without looking). After everyone has drawn from the basket, find the woman whose watch (or other item) you have. Return the item to its owner and take the paper with her "obedient response" on it instead. During the week, pray for the woman whose paper you received and call her to encourage her in her active, obedient faith.

Just for Fun

Plan a time to do a cookie bake together this week. Each of you can bring one or two things: cookie dough (different kinds), frosting/icing, decorations and food coloring, cookie cutters, and so forth, and when the cookies are all baked and decorated you can choose an assortment of different cookies to take with you.

Post a large piece of paper someplace where you all can see it. As you are baking discuss all the areas you can think of in which you had to be "obedient" in order for the cookie bake to happen (going to the cookie bake instead of staying home, bringing your share of the ingredients, etc.). Write these on the paper. As a group, discuss what spiritual applications you draw from this experience. Add these to the poster also.

Praying Together

Stand in a circle and "layer" your hands in the middle (everyone add one hand to the "pile," one at a time). Beginning with the woman whose hand is on top, lift up a one-sentence prayer for the woman who had your watch (and now has your paper with the "obedient response" on it). You might pray that she be bold in her obedience, or that she be blessed or joyful in her active faith. You could ask that she reap the benefits of obedience quickly or that she be able to wait patiently in God's grace. When the first woman is finished praying, the woman whose hand is now on top of the pile can pray for the woman who had her watch, and so on, until all have prayed.

Faith is the daring of the soul to go further than it can see.
WILLIAM NEWTON CLARKE

Making It Real
in Your Own Life

1. Read Psalm 19. Note how in verses 1–6 we see our awesome God through his creation. We can have faith because the object of our faith is this same mighty Lord! In verses 7–11 we see him through his Word, which gives us wisdom, joy, and light. God's Word is also the path of obedience. He doesn't change the rules every day or make us guess what he wants from us. As you think about these truths, write out the last few verses, 12–14, in your own words.

2. Look at Psalm 19 and your paraphrased verses each day this week. Take some time to pray and seek God's direction in your life. In what specific areas is he asking you to step out in faith and obey him?

3. Are you willing to take obedient action? Why or why not?

> *What you do reveals what you believe about God,*
> *regardless of what you say.*
> HENRY BLACKABY

Mary Magdalene: Unwavering Faith

I'm not much of a gardener, I must confess. Oh, I'm pretty good with philodendrons—but then, so is almost any five-year-old with a watering can. I like plants and flowers though, especially bougainvillea and tulips. I am drawn particularly to the desert plants that grow in Arizona where I live, like the prickly pear, saguaro, barrel cactus, and ocotillo. They appear so strong and simple and are unwavering in their focus: "grow!" Because of the light rainfall here, some desert plants send roots deep into the earth for water. Many others have lengthy root systems that are close to the surface so they can soak up even the smallest amount of moisture that falls to the earth.

Is your faith like that: unwavering, focused, determined? Sometimes my faith is as solid as a barrel cactus: immovable, armor in place, growing steadily southward, oblivious to blazing days and freezing nights, growing, growing, growing. At other times I am more like the delicate African violet. The smallest disturbance bruises a leaf; the slightest variance in moisture causes me to shrivel or wilt.

Psalm 1 tells us that the righteous person is like a tree firmly planted by refreshing streams of water. We see a picture of this kind of firm, unwavering faith in Mary Magdalene. What does this woman who followed Jesus have to teach us about our relationship with him?

> *A wavering Christian is a Christian who trusts in the love of God one day and doubts it the next, and who is alternately happy or miserable accordingly.*
>
> HANNAH WHITALL SMITH

A Moment for Quiet Reflection

1. Find a quiet moment to curl up in your favorite chair with your Bible. If the weather's nice, sit outside in the sun! Consider your faith. Is it like a newly planted seed, fervently growing? Perhaps it's a bulb buried in the cold earth, waiting for spring. Or it could be a healthy tree, its roots taking in water and nutrients as it continues to grow strong. Read Psalm 1 and write down the differences between the righteous (those whose faith is in the Lord) and the wicked (those whose faith is in themselves or nonexistent).

2. What suggestions does this psalm give you for how to grow in your faith like the tree planted by water? What are some specific ways you will accomplish this in the week ahead?

3. Bring a small potted plant to this week's study (i.e., the very inexpensive kind you can get at the grocery store that come in tiny plastic pots).

Knowing God's Heart

1. From Luke 8:1–3 we learn that Mary Magdalene was healed of seven demons and that she was one of a group of women who traveled from town to town and used their personal resources to support Jesus and the disciples. Read John 20:10–18 together. What does Mary's use of "my Lord" in verse 13 tell us about her faith?

2. Why do you think Mary didn't recognize Jesus?

3. How does this apply to our faith today?

4. Share with the group a current situation in which you are looking for Jesus but don't recognize his presence. Help each other consider ways in which he is present even when you can't see him.

5. Read John 10:1–9, 14–15. How is this parable illustrated in Mary Magdalene's encounter with Jesus at the tomb?

6. Can you think of a time when you believe Jesus "called you by name" and you followed him because you "knew" his voice? Tell the group about your experience.

7. In John 20:17, what do you think Jesus meant when he told Mary not to hold onto him because he had not yet returned to his Father?

8. Discuss whether or not you think this caused Mary's faith to grow stronger. Do you think your faith would be more unwavering if you had Jesus here with you physically? Why or why not?

9. What were Jesus' final instructions to Mary Magdalene (John 20:17)? How did her response demonstrate her faith in him?

10. How are you demonstrating your own faith in the Lord? Discuss what kind of active obedience you think he is asking of you.

Friendship Boosters

1. Sketch your favorite plant or flower and label it. (You don't have to be an artist; think "modern art" and just have a fast, fun time with it!) Write down one or two ways in which you would like your faith to be like this plant and share them with the group.

2. Break into groups of three. In each group designate a woman to be "earth," one to be "water," and one to be "sun." Have the "earths" give the plants they brought with them to the "waters," the "waters" give their plants to the "suns," and the "suns" give their plants to the "earths." As you care for your new plant in the next week, pray for the woman from whom you received it, and ask God to give her a growing, unwavering faith.

> She (Mary Magdalene) still calls him "my Lord."
> As far as she knows his lips were silent.
> As far as she knows, his corpse had been
> carted off by grave robbers.
> But in spite of it all, he is still her Lord.
> Such devotion moves Jesus. It moves him closer to her....
> "Miriam," he said softly, "surprise!"
> Mary was shocked.
> It's not often you hear your name spoken
> by an eternal tongue.
> But when she did, she recognized it.
> And when she did, she responded correctly.
> She worshipped him.
>
> MAX LUCADO

Just for Fun

During the week ahead, be on the lookout for something that reveals a different perspective on an everyday object or situation. Keep your mind open; it could be anything: a deflated blow-up globe, a picture of a kitten in a fishbowl with a huge goldfish on the outside looking at it, a kaleidoscope. . . . Buy (or make) an inexpensive object that provides a different perspective than usual. Put it in a gift bag or wrap it and bring it to next week's study for a "perspective" exchange.

Praying Together

Remain in your "earth"/"water"/"sun" groups. Jot down the other women's prayer requests regarding unwavering faith. Then have all the "earths" get together, all the "waters" together, and all the "suns" together. In these groups, take turns lifting up the requests from your mixed group.

> *Now Faith . . . is the art of holding on to things your reason has once accepted, in spite of your changing moods. . . . Unless you teach your moods "where they get off," you can never be . . . a sound Christian . . . but just a creature dithering to and fro, with its beliefs really dependent on the weather and the state of its digestion.*
>
> C. S. Lewis

Making It Real
in Your Own Life

1. Read Jeremiah 17:7–8. Spend a few minutes looking at each phrase and noting the blessings of faith. Which one means the most to you right now? Why?

2. Write out the quote below on a piece of paper. Then begin to write it again but, this time, after each line write out its specific applications in your life right now. What are the curves tossed into your life, and what would a calmer faith look like? When you finish, write out a prayer committing to God the areas in which you need unwavering faith. Then keep your eyes open to see how God begins to work in you and in these situations.

> *Yep, a calmer faith....*
> *That's the quiet place within us*
> *where we don't get whiplash every time*
> *life tosses us a curve.*
> *Where we are...moved only by (God).*
> *Where we weep in repentance,*
> *sleep in peace,*
> *live in fullness,*
> *and sing in victory.*
>
> PATSY CLAIRMONT

Martha: Daily Faith

*H*ow easy is it for you to have faith for today? Right this moment? The day-to-day can be so ... well, *daily.* You know, when people ask you how you are and you reply, "Same old merry-go-round, different day." When families demand and obligations loom and burdens overwhelm, faith can seem like a luxury in which you just don't have time or patience to indulge right now, thank you very much, don't call me, I'll call you. Next month.

Is that true about faith: is it something just for the future? Is that true about *your* faith? Have you had a dream or desire die only to have the Lord appear on the scene wanting to revive it? "God, you're too late," you tell him. "But I know that tomorrow, or next year, or in heaven, this desire will be satisfied." After all, you know he is Christ the Lord; nothing is too difficult for him; all things are possible in him. And he is going to make everything better someday ... in the end. So you know it will all be fine then, even if today looks a little bleak.

Yes, at times it's easy to have faith for the future or eternity. But to believe that eternity begins today is asking a bit much. The car is in the shop again, you somehow have to be in three places at one time with an assortment of children and objects in tow, and you are bewilderingly behind in phone calls and correspondence. What does faith have to do with the pressing demands of the here and now? In the face of raw, sometimes painful, reality, where does faith fit in?

A woman named Martha had those same questions. Her brother Lazarus has just died and been buried, the house is full of people, she is in the midst of mourning, and Jesus shows up and wants her to draw on her faith savings account for the future today. *Wait a minute . . . Right now?!* What's a girl to do? Let's take a look and find out.

> *By faith, things future, the things we hope for,*
> *become a present reality.*
>
> RONALD DUNN

A Moment
for Quiet Reflection

1. Get away by yourself and spend some time with Jesus. Your Bible, a cup of tea, a quiet spot in a comfortable chair, just the two of you—bliss! Talk honestly with him about your faith. What is your faith like for today? How does it compare with your faith for tomorrow? Next year? What about three years from now? How is your faith for eternity?

2. Read Psalm 145. Write down the phrases or verses that encourage you in your faith for the here and now. Then write down those that encourage you in your faith for tomorrow. On another piece of paper write your favorite verse from these and a brief note about why it encourages you. Bring this to the next group meeting.

Knowing God's Heart

1. Read John 11:17–27 together. You are probably familiar with the story in Luke 10 about the two sisters, Mary and Martha. While Mary is a "human *being*" and receives praise from Jesus for having "chosen the better part" by sitting at his feet and learning of him, Martha is a "human *doing*," busy cooking and cleaning and complaining that she is doing it all by herself. This apparent contrast in their behavior and personality makes it interesting to read about their roles in this account of their interactions with Jesus after their brother, Lazarus, has died. Before Martha and Jesus even begin their conversation, how is Martha's faith expressed?

2. Martha greets Jesus with some powerful statements. Looking at verses 21 and 22, what do her words reveal about her basic beliefs regarding him?

3. What does Martha seem to be asking Jesus to do here?

4. In verses 23 and 24, is Martha referring to the same time frame that Jesus is talking about? When is Martha's faith for?

5. What timeless truth do you think Jesus is trying to communicate to Martha?

6. What do Jesus' words to Martha mean to you personally today—right now and for the future?

7. Have someone read verse 27 aloud. What enabled Martha to make this tremendous statement?

8. Read John 11:38–44. Think of a current situation that challenges your faith. Share with one another the ways in which your faith is like Martha's: strong one minute and nonexistent the next.

9. What was necessary to renew Martha's faith when it began to waver?

10. Discuss a time when you needed this kind of reminder or encouragement from Jesus, and got it.

11. What blessings did Martha reap because of her faith? What blessings might result from your faith, right now and up the road?

The great need is not to do things, but to believe things.
OSWALD CHAMBERS

Friendship Boosters

1. Share a situation in which your faith is stronger for tomorrow than it is for today. Avoid judging, advising, or patronizing others; instead practice listening to one another with love and empathy.

2. Take out the paper with the Psalm 145 verse and your note. Make sure your name and number is on it. Sit or stand in a circle, crumple your papers, and toss them high into the center of the circle. As the papers come down, grab one. (If you get your own, throw it right back up in the air for someone else to catch!) During the week, pray for the woman whose paper you received and call to encourage her to have faith for today, perhaps using your own favorite verse from Psalm 145 and personal life experiences in which God was faithful to you.

Just for Fun

Have a "perspective object" exchange with the objects you collected in response to last week's "Just for Fun" activity. For as many objects as there are, put numbers in a "hat" (for instance, if there are eight objects, put slips of paper, numbered one through eight, into the hat). Then have each woman who brought an object draw a number. The first woman can pick any gift object she chooses. The second woman can pick a new object, or take the first woman's choice. (Remember, each Psalm 145 verse stays with the same object it came with!) If she takes the first woman's choice, the first woman gets to choose again. Then the woman who drew number three may choose either a new object, or an object from the first or second woman, and so on, until all the women have chosen. An object may not change hands more than twice (meaning that the third woman who chooses it keeps it!) You might want to have drinks and snacks as you discuss the question, "How do you think God wants to change your perspective?" As you wrap up your study of faith, take the perspective gift you received and the verse from Psalm 145 and meditate on it in the weeks ahead.

Praying Together

Continue to sit or stand in your circle. Join hands if you like. Have someone begin the prayer with the first two verses of Psalm 145: "We will exalt you, our God the King; we will praise your name for ever and ever. Every day we will praise you and extol your name for ever and ever." Then, one at a time, toss in one-word praises about God (for example, for his "faithfulness," "love," "Jesus," and so forth). When it slows down have someone ready to end with the last verse from Psalm 145: "Our mouths will speak in praise of the Lord. Let every creature praise his holy name for ever and ever. Amen."

> *The function of faith is to turn God's promises into facts.*
> J. OSWALD SANDERS

Making It Real
in Your Own Life

1. Read Jeremiah 29:11–14. What promises does the Lord make to his people?

2. Do these promises apply to you today? Why or why not?

3. According to verses 12 and 13, what are God's promises contingent upon?

4. According to Matthew 7:7–11, what happens when you seek the Lord with faith and diligence?

5. What specific thing do you want to ask God for today? Ask in faith and be ready to recognize the ways in which he answers in the here and now.

> *Self will turns the eyes on self*
> *and what self strongly wants.*
> *Faith turns the eyes on Christ to ask*
> *Him what He wants.*
> *Self will worries about the results.*
> *Faith worries only about obedience,*
> *then leaves the result to Jesus.*
>
> CATHERINE MARSHALL

LEADER'S GUIDE

LESSON ONE

1. The Pharisee was a respected member of the community, while the woman was a former prostitute as well as an uninvited guest. A rabbi, which is what Jesus was considered, did not normally speak with women in public, never mind ex-prostitutes! To top it all off, her attentions created quite a scene as her tears spilled onto his feet, which she then wiped with her hair and kissed before she broke the costly alabaster jar and poured the expensive ointment over Jesus' feet. All in all, it must have caused quite a stir! And Jesus not only accepts it but praises her for it and rebukes Simon the Pharisee. Jesus does not look down on women as inferior beings, and no sin is too great for him to forgive. Any woman, including you, can approach him boldly and receive lavish love and forgiveness.

2. The sinful woman exhibits a greater faith in Jesus in the way she is completely focused on him and doesn't care what anyone else thinks. She is extravagant not only in her material sacrifice, but also in her artless display of emotion and humility. The Pharisee is very conscious of appearances and social conventions, yet he neglects even minimal social courtesies such as providing water for Jesus to wash his feet when he arrives. He is a picture of spiritual blindness and false pride.

4. The woman went to Jesus perhaps because in true repentance she knew she could find grace and forgiveness in him. How radical her faith must have been to compel her to go where she knew she would not be welcome by the other guests!

6. When Jesus pronounced her forgiven and told her that her faith had saved her, she must have felt great love for and peace in him. She found what she was so desperately looking for, and what we still look for today. We don't know what happened to this woman after she left Simon's house, but we can presume that Jesus' response had an immediate, as well as future, impact on her life.

Friendship Boosters. Five-by-eight index cards make good name tags and can easily be read across a circle! Write each woman's name in bold on one side. Staple a piece of wide ribbon to the top, with a safety pin through it to attach it to a shirt. On the back of each card, write your name and phone number.

LESSON TWO

1. Despite the fact that she was barren (and this was considered a serious personal failing in the Israelite community) Elizabeth lived a life pleasing to God and observed all his commandments and regulations. Scripture tells us she was beyond childbearing age, yet despite her many years of personal disappointment, she remained faithful to God throughout this time.

2. Elizabeth didn't complain about being pregnant at her age, or wonder why the Lord couldn't have done this for her when she was young. She gave him praise and glory and gratitude for showing her his favor in his time. She recognized that he is God and is holy and just and righteous in all that he does.

3. It was not social convention that dictated this time. Possibly, in her gladness, Elizabeth had a desire to be alone with the Lord and went into seclusion simply to spend time with him and to praise him in joy and thankfulness for what he had done for her.

5. Elizabeth once again showed that she didn't feel unfairly treated by God. Although she was older, she didn't presume to think she should have been the one to have the honor of bearing the Messiah. She greeted Mary with love and respect and recognized Mary as the mother of her Lord. By the power of the Holy Spirit, she believed Mary and didn't rebuke or judge her for her unmarried, pregnant condition. Furthermore, she opened up her home to Mary during the last trimester of her own miracle pregnancy.

6. Elizabeth had an intimate relationship with the Lord and upon Mary's arrival she was filled with the Holy Spirit due, no doubt, to the time she spent with the Lord.

   Mary's situation was not a normal, everyday situation, and Elizabeth's response was not a normal, everyday response. Despite the fantastic circumstances of Mary's pregnancy, Elizabeth believed and even, apparently, had some foreknowledge of the incredible event. If she hadn't had an intimate relationship with the Lord and deep faith in him, she wouldn't have been able to respond this way.

8. Elizabeth named the baby John, as the angel Gabriel directed. Verse 61 tells us that there was no one in her family with that name. Very often a son was named in honor of some relative, particularly his father, as is still true today. To obey the angel Gabriel was to name their first and only child with a name out of nowhere, after no one in particular. This showed great faith on Elizabeth's part in the Lord and in his messenger, Gabriel, as well as in the angel's promises for this special child. "John" means "the Lord is gracious," and in giving that name to her precious son, she showed she believed her Lord was gracious indeed. She was

firm about this decision, even when her neighbors and relatives questioned her and suggested the baby be named after his father and then they turned to Zechariah, in his mute state, and asked him about it!

LESSON THREE

1. While Sarai's action was disobedient to God, it was the result of faith in his promise. He had said that Abram would have a son; perhaps she had been mistaken when she thought it would be with her.

4. After waiting all these years and now being well past childbearing age, Abraham and Sarah may have felt that God was simply teasing them with these promises. They both laughed at the promise. Their laughter was of ridicule and pain at having their hope dangled before them once again.

LESSON FOUR

1. When Naomi heard the Lord had provided food for his people, she prepared to return home. She prayed the Lord would show kindness to her daughters-in-law. She prayed the Lord would provide each of them another husband. She displayed a very matter-of-fact faith. Perhaps the fact that she was gracious and willing to "let go" of these two women and return home alone rather than manipulate or cling to them as "all she had left" was also evidence of her faith that God would take care of her, even though she had lost her husband and sons in Moab.

2. Orpah chooses all that is familiar: she returns to her home and her gods. Ruth steps out in faith and chooses to remain with Naomi, to make Naomi's people her people, and to make Naomi's God her God. Verse 17 shows her total commitment to her declaration in verse 16.

4. There is no such thing as "luck" or "coincidence" in God's economy! His divine hand is on his children and their circumstances always. Consider the stories of Joseph in Egypt (Gen. 37 and following; see Gen. 50:20), Moses and Pharaoh (Exod. 3 and following; see Exod. 12:36; Prov. 16:9; Jer. 10:23), and Jesus' crucifixion (see Acts 2:22–24; Phil. 2:13). As is plain from the outcome, both as we finish reading in Ruth and as God's story continues to unfold through the Bible, Ruth's ending up in Boaz's field was part of God's divine plan.

6. Ruth trusted that Naomi would not ask her to do anything unseemly or inappropriate. As she unquestioningly followed her mother-in-law to Bethlehem, she obeyed her in this situation also. Having committed herself to this Lord in whom Naomi had faith, she didn't turn back.

8. Naomi was confident that Boaz would handle the situation properly and tells Ruth to wait. Ruth has displayed a calm, obedient faith all through this story and so we can imagine that she was able to wait in quiet expectation for Boaz to settle the matter. She didn't take things into her own

hands and seemed to have faith that the Lord would take care of everything for her. *Levirate marriage:* This widespread custom is first witnessed in Genesis 38. The terms are spelled out in Deuteronomy 25. Basically, if a man had a brother who died and left his widow childless, it was the man's duty to marry her and to name their first son for the deceased brother. The son would be an heir to the dead man and therefore inherit his estate. This marriage custom is the basis of the more complicated levirate marriage we read of in Ruth.

10. In the Jewish culture, children were considered a gift from the Lord, and sons were especially a blessing because the family name and property were handed down through males.

    Barrenness was a reproach, as we learn from other biblical accounts (i.e., Sarah, Hannah, Elizabeth). In addition, an Israelite woman had the hope that God would choose her to bear the promised Messiah, for whom the Israelites were always looking. The birth of this baby boy was a gift from God and a sign of his love and blessing.

11. Naomi is blessed by the birth of this baby, Obed, who was the heir who replaced Naomi's firstborn son. Obed was also King David's grandfather. Boaz, Ruth, and Obed are also ultimately part of the genealogy of Jesus Christ, the unequaled Redeemer.

    Friendship Boosters. Have a basket (or something similar) on hand to use in the second activity.

    Just for Fun. Have a poster-size piece of paper taped to the kitchen wall. Some areas in which everyone had to be obedient include having to be disciplined and follow directions; not being able just to do whatever you felt like doing, such as sitting at home watching TV instead of getting your stuff together and heading out the door on time, or turning left toward the mall instead of right toward the house where the cookie bake was to be held; heeding the oven timer and taking out the cookies on time, even if that meant interrupting a fascinating conversation!

LESSON FIVE

1. Despite the bleak appearance of the situation, Mary Magdalene still had faith that Jesus was her personal Lord. Her faith did not die with her Savior.

2. One practical reason why Mary didn't recognize Jesus might have been that her eyes were filled with tears, or it was still early enough that the light was dim. Jesus might have looked different, too, or he might have kept her from recognizing him until she was ready for the revelation. There were several occasions after his resurrection when he was not recognized by his friends and disciples.

3. There are times today when we do not recognize Jesus' presence in our lives. We might have faith in him but fail to see him because of our tears or the "dimness" of our personal situation. However, that does not mean he isn't with us; he promises never to leave us or forsake us!

5. Jesus was Mary's Lord; she belonged to him. When he called her by name she immediately recognized his voice: he was her Shepherd, she was one of his cherished sheep.

7. Jesus told Mary to "let go" of him and allow him to complete his Father's will. He may also have been establishing the order of their new relationship: it was not going to be like the former human relationship; from then on she would be relating to Jesus as Son of God rather than Son of Man. Once he was ascended into heaven she would be in his presence in a spiritual sense and would not be able to touch him.

9. He told her to go tell the disciples that he was returning to his Father (and theirs). She showed her faith in him by believing his words and obeying his instructions. (In other gospel accounts we learn that the disciples did not believe these various testimonies of the women. Mary was responsible for obeying the Lord; she was not responsible for the disciples' response.)

LESSON SIX

1. As soon as Martha hears that Jesus is coming, she goes out to meet him (verse 20). Mary stays at home and does not greet Jesus until she hears that he's asking for her.

2. She believed that Jesus' power was such that had he been there earlier, Lazarus would not have died. She also believed that Jesus' relationship with the Father was such that whatever he asked of God, he would receive.

3. While it's not explicitly stated, it seems that Martha could have been asking Jesus to ask God to raise her brother from the dead: "But I know that *even now*, God will give you whatever you ask."

4. Although she had just seemed to be hinting that Jesus could ask that Lazarus be raised from the dead right now, when Jesus declares that her brother will rise again, meaning that day, Martha expresses confident belief only that he will be raised at the *last* day, when all believers would be resurrected. Her faith is for what God will do in the future.

5. Jesus wanted Martha to see that he himself is greater than life and death. He doesn't just give resurrection and life, he *is* the resurrection and the life, and therefore death has no hold over him. In him we have true life; death will not be final for us either.

7. Martha recognized that Jesus was the Messiah, the Son of God. This incredible declaration shows that Martha was a woman of great faith

who knew she was speaking to the God of the universe who could do anything he pleased.

9. Martha needed to be reminded of Jesus' promise: she would see the glory of God if she believed. Discuss how Jesus himself graciously encourages us to remain strong when our faith wavers.

11. When Martha trusted Jesus' promise and allowed the stone to be removed, her beloved brother was brought back to life and restored to the family. Discuss the spiritual blessings Martha must have received from witnessing this miracle. (For example, her faith in God's power was no doubt strengthened; her confidence that Jesus was the Messiah was affirmed; she experienced a very personal expression of God's love for her.)

FAITH

Women of Faith Bible studies are based on the popular
Women of Faith conferences.

Women of Faith is partnering with Zondervan Publishing House,
Integrity Music, *Today's Christian Woman* magazine, and Campus Crusade
to offer conferences, publications, worship music, and inspirational gifts
that support and encourage today's Christian women.

Since their beginning in January of 1996, the Women of Faith conferences
have enjoyed an enthusiastic welcome by women across the country.

Call 1-888-49-FAITH for the many conference locations and dates available.

www.women-of-faith.com

**See the following page for additional information
about Women of Faith products.**

Look for these faith-building resources from Women of Faith:

Friends Through Thick & Thin by Gloria Gaither, Peggy Benson,
  Sue Buchanan, and Joy Mackenzie
  Hardcover 0-310-21726-1

We Brake for Joy! by Patsy Clairmont, Barbara Johnson, Marilyn Meberg,
  Luci Swindoll, Sheila Walsh, and Thelma Wells
  Hardcover 0-310-22042-4

Bring Back the Joy by Sheila Walsh
  Hardcover 0-310-22023-8
  Audio Pages 0-310-22222-2

The Joyful Journey by Patsy Clairmont, Barbara Johnson,
  Marilyn Meberg, and Luci Swindoll
  Softcover 0-310-22155-2
  Audio Pages 0-310-21454-8

Joy Breaks by Patsy Clairmont, Barbara Johnson,
  Marilyn Meberg, and Luci Swindoll
  Hardcover 0-310-21345-2

Women of Faith Journal
  Journal 0-310-97634-0

Promises of Joy for Women of Faith
  Gift Book 0-310-97389-9

Words of Wisdom for a Woman of Faith
  Gift Book 0-310-97390-2

Prayers for a Woman of Faith
  Gift Book 0-310-97336-8